HERNANDO DE SOTO

HERNANDO DE SOTO

Great Explorers of the World

Spanish Conquistador in the Americas

Jeff C. Young

Enslow Publishers, Inc.
40 Industrial Road
Box 398
Berkeley Heights, NJ 07922
USA

http://www.enslow.com

To my good friend and erstwhile faculty colleague, Steve Hughes

Library of Congress Cataloging-in-Publication Data

Young, Jeff C., 1948–
   Hernando de Soto : Spanish conquistador in the Americas / Jeff C.
Young.
        p. cm. — (Great Explorers of the world)
   Includes bibliographical references and index.
   Summary: "Discusses the life of Spanish explorer Hernando de Soto,
including his travels in the Americas, the claim of Florida for Spain,
and his eventual discovery of the Mississippi River"—Provided by
publisher.
   ISBN-13: 978-1-59845-104-7 (alk. paper)
   ISBN-10: 1-59845-104-9 (alk. paper)
   1. Soto, Hernando de, ca. 1500-1542—Juvenile literature. 2.
Explorers—America—Biography—Juvenile literature. 3. Explorers—
Spain—Biography—Juvenile literature. 4. America—Discovery and
exploration—Spanish—Juvenile literature. 5. Southern States—
Discovery and exploration—Spanish—Juvenile literature. 6. Mississippi
River—Discovery and exploration—Spanish—Juvenile literature. I. Title.
   E125.S7Y68 2009
   970.01'6092—dc22
   [B]
                            2008030753

Printed in the United States of America

10 9 8 7 6 5 4 3 2 1

To Our Readers: We have done our best to make sure all Internet Addresses in this book were active and appropriate when we went to press. However, the author and the publisher have no control over and assume no liability for the material available on those Internet sites or on other Web sites they may link to. Any comments or suggestions can be sent by e-mail to comments@enslow.com or to the address on the back cover.

♻ Enslow Publishers, Inc., is committed to printing our books on recycled paper. The paper in every book contains 10% to 30% post-consumer waste (PCW). The cover board on the outside of each book contains 100% PCW. Our goal is to do our part to help young people and the environment too!

Illustration Credits: Enslow Publishers, Inc., pp. 12, 69; The Granger Collection, New York, pp. 3, 10, 22, 29, 52, 58–59, 61, 64–65, 66, 95, 100, 103; Library of Congress, pp. 76–77, 82, 86; National Park Service, p. 62; © René Byrskov 2007, p. 104 © Shutterstock®, p. 44.

Ship Illustration Used in Chapter Openers: © Jupiterimages Corporation.

Cover Illustration: The Granger Collection, New York (Portrait of Hernando de Soto).

Contents

Explorer Timeline

1500—Hernando de Soto is born in the Extremadura region in western Spain.

1514—Probably sails to Panama as a member of Pedrarias Davila's expedition.

1519—Serves as a field captain during Juan de Espinosa's conquest of western Panama.

1524—Serves as a field captain during Francisco Hernandez de Cordoba's conquest of Nicaragua; settles in Nicaragua as a mine operator.

1528—Becomes a wealthy landowner and business-man in Nicaragua.

1531—Serves as an officer under Francisco Pizarro; helps Pizarro conquer the Inca in Peru; is richly rewarded for his assistance.

1534—Named the Spanish lieutenant governor of Cuzco, Peru.

1536—Returns to Spain as a famous military leader and a very wealthy man; receives a hero's welcome.

1537—Spanish king Charles V gives de Soto a con-tract to explore, colonize, and conquer lands in North America.

1538—De Soto and his army leave Spain for Cuba and then Florida.

1539—De Soto reaches the west coast of Florida and claims it as a Spanish possession.

1539—De Soto and his army spend the winter at
–1540 Apalachee, Florida.

1540—*October 18:* De Soto's army defeats American Indians at the Battle of Mabila.

1541—*May 8:* De Soto reaches the banks of the Mississippi River. He and his army cross the river on June 18.

1542—*May 21:* Dies near the Mississippi River.

1543—*July 2:* Surviving members of de Soto's expedition sail down the Mississippi River to the Gulf of Mexico.

—*September 10:* Expedition arrives at Veracruz, Mexico.

Chapter 1

A Sight to See

When Hernando de Soto came to a strange new land looking for silver and gold, he did not find them. What he found forever links his name with a river that became America's chief inland waterway—the Mississippi River.

Nearly two years of constant marching and fighting had weakened and wearied Spanish explorer Hernando de Soto and his army. He had marched his soldiers over unfamiliar and un-friendly terrain, wading through swamps, fording rivers and streams, and fighting American Indians. Since landing in Florida in May 1539, they had marched more than fifteen hundred miles in search of riches that still eluded them.

For eight days, they had been lost and aimlessly wandering through a wilderness of towering trees—pines, magnolias, maples, and oaks. Their meager food supplies were steadily dwindling. About one-fifth of Hernando de Soto's original army of 650 men had perished in the past two years. They had died from disease, starvation, exhaustion, and battle wounds.

HERHANDO DE SOTO:

*Estremeño: uno de los descubridores y conquis-
tadores del Perú: recorrió toda la Florida y venció á
sus naturales invencibles hasta entonces: murió
en su expedición el año de 1543. á los 42. de su edad.*

On the morning of May 8, 1541, de Soto was marching at the head of his army when he saw the outline of the huge river. He raised one hand to signal the army to stop. Soon, he stood on a low bluff overlooking the Mississippi, a vast, swirling expanse of muddy water.

One account claims that de Soto fell to his knees and thanked God for allowing him to make such an incredible discovery. After giving thanks, de Soto and his army continued their march. Their pace quickened as they descended a lengthy, gradual slope. When they reached the river's eastern bank, they were awestruck by the waterway's immense width. The river was at least one mile wide. For de Soto, it represented one more challenge to meet and one more obstacle to overcome.

Now that he had found this river, he had to cross it and conquer the lands beyond. In de Soto's mind the riches he had failed to find were waiting on the other side of the Mississippi. Surely some fabled golden city or empire was there for the taking in the interior of this strange, unfamiliar land. In truth, the city of gold existed only in fables and folklore.

As soon as he found a suitable campsite, de Soto ordered his men to build rafts to take them across the deep, wide river. By mid-June they had built four large rafts, complete with sails and oars. Within a few hours, they were on the river's other

CANADA

NORTH DAKOTA

Lake Itasca
(Source of the Mississippi River)

Lake Superior

MINNESOTA

MICHIGAN

SOUTH DAKOTA

WISCONSIN

Minnesota River

Mississippi River

Wisconsin River

Lake Michigan

Lake Huron

MICHIGAN

NEBRASKA

Des Moines River

IOWA

Mississippi River

Illinois River

OHIO

KANSAS

Missouri River

ILLINOIS

INDIANA

Ohio River

MISSOURI

KENTUCKY

OKLAHOMA

ARKANSAS

Arkansas River

Mississippi River

TENNESSEE

Cumberland River

Tennessee River

N
W   E
S

TEXAS

Red River

ALABAMA

GEORGIA

MISSISSIPPI

LOUISIANA

FLORIDA

Mississippi Delta

Gulf of Mexico

MEXICO

Hernando de Soto's discovery of the Mississippi, the largest river in North America, opened an important trade route for European colonists. This is a present-day map of the river in the United States.

side. They were on the banks of the Mississippi in present-day Arkansas. De Soto prepared his army for more marching. Now it was time for de Soto to claim riches and land for Spain. He had traveled thousands of miles from Spain to find wealth. But would he find what he was looking for?

Chapter 2

A Teenager in the Army

The explorer Hernando de Soto was born in a country and culture that revered soldiers. Historians believed that he was born in 1500, although there are no documents to confirm this. Historians also dispute his place of birth, but de Soto claimed that he was born in the Spanish town of Jerez de los Caballeros, about seventy miles northwest of Seville. According to one biographer, several of de Soto's friends and relatives supported that claim.

DE SOTO'S SPAIN

When de Soto was born, Spain had been almost continually at war for more than seven centuries. In A.D. 711, Berbers, Arabs, and other people of the Muslim faith conquered most of the country. In the early 1000s, internal conflicts destroyed the unified Muslim government that had ruled most of Spain. The country separated into many small Muslim states and some independent cities.

Also during the 1000s, groups of Christians in northern Spain, which had remained independent after the Muslim conquest pushed the Muslims southward.

Castile became the most powerful of the Christian kingdoms, and their leader, El Cid, freed Valenica from the Moors (Spanish Muslims). Today, Spaniards still honor El Cid as one of their country's greatest national heroes.

By the late 1200s, the Christians had gained control of most of Spain. The Muslim territory was reduced to the kingdom of Granada in southern Spain. Throughout the 1300s and the greater part of the 1400s, Castile controlled most of Spain. The marriage of Prince Ferdinand of Aragon and Princess Isabella of Castile in 1469 put most of Spain under the rule of a monarchy.

By 1512, Ferdinand had united Spain under his rule. In the process, he had driven out the Muslims and the Spanish Jews who refused to convert to Christianity. By that time, de Soto was a skilled horseman and was probably aspiring to become a soldier and explorer.

JOINING THE ARMY

When he was in his early teens, de Soto was reputed to be stronger and taller than most grown men. His family was poor but well-respected in their community. Hernando was one of at least four children and he had learned to do things for himself. Since he had little formal education and little money, his job options were limited. His two major choices were manual labor or military service. The dreariness and drudgery of manual labor could not compete with the glamour and adventure of being a soldier.

When and how de Soto left home is unknown. Most historians believe that it happened in 1513 or 1514. He traveled to Seville and joined an expedition of two thousand colonists commanded by Pedrarias Davila. De Soto and the other adventurers had been lured by reports of abundant gold deposits in the New World region of Panama.

King Ferdinand ordered and sponsored the expedition. Since Christopher Columbus's first voyage in 1492, King Ferdinand and Queen Isabella had been sponsoring expeditions to start Spanish colonies in the New World. In 1493, they had Columbus lead 1,200 settlers to the present-day Dominican Republic, where they founded Santo Domingo. It became the first permanent European settlement in the Western Hemisphere.

After the Spanish had founded Santo Domingo, they used the new settlement as a base to conquer Puerto Rico and Cuba. Their conquests took a heavy toll on the Spanish settlers who had come there hoping for sudden wealth from the rich gold deposits. Caribbean Indian attacks, disease, hunger, and the failure to adapt to the rigors of the sweltering tropical climate claimed the lives of hundreds of Spanish settlers.

But the Indians in the New World suffered much higher casualties. Warfare, the harsh forced labor of their enslavement by the Spanish, and new diseases brought over from Europe killed hundreds of thousands of Indians.

DE SOTO JOINS BALBOA

In 1511 and 1512, the Spanish explorer and soldier Vasco Nuñez de Balboa sent letters to King Ferdinand describing Panama as a land teeming with rich deposits of gold, fertile soil, and peaceful Indians who could easily be subdued and enslaved. Balboa claimed that there were at least fifty streams containing gold with "large lumps in great abundance."[1]

Balboa assured his King that Spain could claim these vast riches if Ferdinand would provide Balboa with weapons and a thousand-man army. Along with gaining and amassing the country's boundless riches, Spain would be conquering "a great part of the world."[2]

Balboa's claims were greatly exaggerated, but King Ferdinand believed them. In May 1513, he ordered that a great armada, or fleet of ships, be prepared as soon as possible. The original plan was for eight hundred colonists to board nine vessels, but the expedition grew to more than two thousand settlers and eighteen vessels. The size of the undertaking caused it to be delayed until April 1514.

Presumably, de Soto was on board one of the eighteen ships during the two-and-a-half-month voyage from Spain to Panama. Since he held the rank of a page, or a mere soldier, most of his time was spent below the main deck in the hold of the ship. He was probably confined to cramped quarters with other men, supplies, chickens, goats, and horses. He slept in whatever space on the floor he could claim for himself. Occasionally, he would be allowed to stand on the main deck to breathe in some fresh air and escape the cramped space belowdecks.

In early June 1514, the fleet dropped anchor at the Gulf of Santa Marta on the northern coast of Colombia. Davila had his army burn Indian huts and capture and enslave the survivors. The soldiers seized any gold trinkets they found. They massacred any Indians who tried to resist. The carnage continued for three days. It ended only when the invaders set sail for Panama.

● Gold in Panama?

On June 26, 1514, most of the armada landed at the Gulf of Urabá in Panama. There is no record of whether anyone was on shore to greet the colonists. There is also no record of the colonists' reaction to their first glimpse of Panama. However, historians believe that the Spaniards were stunned and disappointed by what they saw.

When they crowded on the decks of the ships, they saw stretches of a sandy beach bordered by dense growths of canes and large palm trees. In the background, fog partially obscured the six-thousand-foot peaks of the Darien Mountains. There were no well-built houses, buildings, or docks. What was supposed to be a tropical paradise teeming with gold deposits looked like a dangerous wilderness.

There was a small settlement where they landed. It was called Santa Maria la Antigua del Darien. It consisted of about one hundred or so huts built by earlier Spanish settlers. But the new settlers arrived there shortly after a plague of locusts had decimated the colony's food supply.

The oppressive humidity and tropical heat overwhelmed the colonists. To their dismay, swarms of mosquitoes, lured by the scent of the colonists' sweat, set upon them. Still, they endured the many hardships because of the lure and promise of gold.

After returning to Spain from his fourth voyage in 1502, Columbus had reported that the interior of the Isthmus of Panama contained "a vast quantity of gold."[3] But, Columbus's report was not based on having seen any gold deposits. His information came from Indians he had met.

Then in 1504, a mapmaker and explorer named Juan de la Cosa plundered some gold jewelry, idols, and kettledrums from Indians living on Panama's eastern shore. The small amount of gold he seized was probably brought into Panama by traders. It is likely that the gold originated in Peru or Colombia. But, de la Cosa's spoils and Columbus's claims were cited as evidence of vast Panamanian gold deposits.

The greed for gold was so great that the Spanish overlooked the fact that practically everyone in Columbus's and de la Cosa's expeditions died. In two other recent expeditions, more than seven hundred men perished, while the Spaniards collected hardly any gold.

BALBOA'S ACHIEVEMENT

When de Soto arrived in Panama, the Spanish had but one positive achievement in Panama. Explorer Vasco Nuñez de Balboa and his band of five hundred men had succeeded in establishing a colony.

Balboa had first come to the New World in 1501, when he joined a Spanish expedition to South America. After exploring the area around the Gulf of Urabá in present-day Colombia, the expedition sailed on to the island of Hispaniola. (Today, that island is composed of two nations— Haiti and the Dominican Republic.) Balboa settled in Hispaniola.

In 1509, he attempted to join the first Spanish expedition to establish a colony in South America.

Balboa was forced to stay in Hispaniola because he was unable to repay money that he had borrowed from other settlers. His debtors refused to let him leave the island. But Balboa found a way to sneak off of the island.

In 1510, Balboa arrived at the Spanish settlement of San Sebastian as a stowaway on a supply ship. The settlement was located in the northwest area of present-day Colombia. At that time, most of the original settlers of San Sebastian had already abandoned the settlement. Indian attacks and a lack of food had forced them out.

Under Balboa's leadership, the new settlers from the supply ship and the survivors of the San Sebastian settlement united. Balboa was likely chosen as their leader because of his prior experience in exploring the area. He knew that the Indians on the west side of the gulf were friendlier and more docile. There Balboa moved the colonists to that area and established the town of

Balboa took possession of the Pacific Ocean for Spain on September 29, 1513.

Santa Maria la Antigua del Darien, known today simply as Darien.

Balboa became the acting governor of Darien, and by the end of 1510, King Ferdinand formally approved his authority. He then led expeditions of conquest. His conquests extended westward into the interior of Panama. By using force, diplomacy, and terrorism, Balboa conquered and enslaved some Indians while making pacts with others.

Reinforcements from Spain and Hispaniola strengthened Balboa's expeditions. He and his soldiers amassed hoards of gold ornaments. During Balboa's conquests, the Indians told him tales of a land called Tubanama, which contained vast deposits of gold. The fabled land was located beyond the mountains and near a great sea.

Balboa's quest to find this gold-rich land led him to become the first European to gaze upon the Pacific Ocean. Balboa called the ocean the South Sea and claimed the huge body of water and all the lands it touched for King Ferdinand.

But while Balboa was exploring Panama and claiming vast expanses of water and land, Davila was plotting against him. Davila had heard of Balboa's successful expeditions, and he was jealous of that success. After Balboa's discovery of the Pacific Ocean, Davila seized Balboa's house and property. Davila also sent a letter to King

Ferdinand suggesting that Diego de Nicuesa deserved credit for discovering the Pacific.

Davila's feelings about Balboa were well founded. Balboa had written the king and said that Davila was doing a poor job as governor. He offered to serve as Davila's replacement.

In March 1515, edicts from King Ferdinand arrived via ship. The king bestowed several honors on Balboa, which intensified Davila's jealousy and insecurity. The monarch appointed Balboa to serve as governor of Coiba and Panama. King Ferdinand further ordered Davila to "favor"[4] Balboa and to "look after him as someone who has also served us."[5]

The King left Davila in charge of all the Spanish colonies in the region. That gave him the authority to prevent the popular Balboa from taking over. In the autumn of 1515, another ship arrived with the news that King Ferdinand was gravely ill. The news emboldened Davila to take decisive action against Balboa. He had Balboa arrested and charged with treason.

Before a trial could commence, the bitter rivals reached an uneasy truce. They arranged a marriage between Balboa and one of Davila's daughters in Spain. Even though they became related by marriage, the two proud, powerful, and ambitious men still could not get along.

By 1518, Balboa was on another voyage of conquest and exploration. Historians believe that de Soto participated in some, if not all, of Balboa's missions into Panama, Colombia, and the Pearl Islands off the coast of Nicaragua. The expedition ended after Davila summoned Balboa to see him. Like an obedient subject and son-in-law, Balboa answered the summons.

Davila had Balboa arrested on false charges of rebellion. The arrest was followed by a swift trial. There was never any doubt about the verdict. In January 1519, Balboa and four of his supporters were beheaded.

A Lesson Learned

During the execution, de Soto and other members of Balboa's expedition were encamped on the Pearl Islands awaiting news of their leader's fate. No record exists of how de Soto reacted when he learned of Balboa's execution. But the news likely shaped his attitudes about the exercise of power.

Since arriving in the New World, de Soto had often witnessed and absorbed the simple lesson that, in the New World, might made right. The strong exploited the weak, and the strong stayed in power by vanquishing their enemies. Greed, intolerance, and cruelty were tolerable if they ultimately brought one great wealth, he believed.

It was a lesson that he would always remember and put into practice. De Soto would use it when he joined Francisco Pizarro's expedition.

Chapter 3

Adventures in Central America

After Balboa was executed, de Soto joined an expedition to western Panama. Gaspar de Espinosa led the expedition. Espinosa had an army of about 150 soldiers. De Soto served as a cavalryman and probably had the rank of field captain. The army's job was to collect slaves and food, and plunder the area for whatever gold they could find.

● DE SOTO PROVES HIS WORTH

When Espinosa and his army reached the first village along their route, he spoke to the Indians' chief, who was named Susa. Espinosa demanded an unconditional surrender and told Susa that his subjects had to turn over all of their treasures and then submit themselves to a life of slavery. Susa and his people fled into the nearby mountains.

At first, Espinosa offered them gifts and sent messages of goodwill. He hoped to earn their trust so they would leave the mountains. When those efforts failed, Espinosa ordered his soldiers to hunt them down and capture them. The soldiers captured Susa and hundreds of his subjects and led them away in chains.

The invaders also took gold treasure estimated to be worth around thirty-three thousand pesos. The soldiers took most of it from entombed bodies. The gold included armor, jewelry, and various trinkets.

De Soto probably got his first taste of plundered gold from one of these tombs. The gold came from a chief named Paris. According to an account by historian Carl Sauer, Paris's entombed body "was decked with gold ornaments from the helmeted head to gold bands about his legs."[1]

Historians believe that de Soto received up to one hundred gold pesos after the soldiers defiled the chief's burial place. But for a soldier in his late teens, it seemed like a fortune. It was probably more than what de Soto's parents in Spain earned in one year.

In October 1519, de Soto and the other surviving members of Espinosa's expedition returned to the new town of Panama City, Panama. De Soto only stayed there for a short time. Espinosa was planning another expedition. The lure of more gold and the excitement of more soldiering were irresistible. In 1520, de Soto joined another expedition into western Panama.

Espinosa's plans were to expand the Spanish sphere of influence in the area and to investigate rumors of a large hidden cache of gold.

DEBELLATOR · FRANCISCUS PIZARRUS · PERUVIA ·

De Soto served with Francisco Pizarro when he was on Espinosa's expedition.

Espinosa divided his army into two groups. The main group sailed under Espinosa's command. Captain Francisco Pizarro led the second group of about one hundred soldiers and traveled on foot.

The second unit was further divided into a main army and a unit called a vanguard, which was under de Soto's command. De Soto led his vanguard of about thirty soldiers for several days across the foothills of the Tabasara Mountains. Then their march halted when they heard shouts and noises of a battle just ahead of them.

De Soto knew that Espinosa's main army may have been in the immediate area. De Soto ordered his men to move forward quickly. He rode to a place that overlooked a valley and was shocked at what he saw. A large group of Indians led by their chief, Urraca, had surrounded and pinned down Espinosa's army.

The ambushed army was trapped in a gully. De Soto could have retreated and summoned Pizarro to send reinforcements. That would have been the safest option. But de Soto decided to act boldly, despite the danger. He ordered his vanguard to attack a fighting force that outnumbered them by about thirty to one.

The unexpected attack frightened and confused the Indians. They probably believed that de Soto was commanding a much larger army. The

Indians halted their attack long enough to give Espinosa's army time to retreat to their ships.

Espinosa and his forces sailed to the small settlement of Nata. He left de Soto and fifty soldiers in Nata under the command of Francisco Companon. Almost as soon as Espinosa and his army left, Urraca and his warriors attacked the unit in Nata.

The overwhelmed soldiers retreated behind the protective shelter of Nata's palisades. Companon quickly realized that his forces were hopelessly outnumbered. Their scant supplies of food and ammunition were going to last only a short time. Companon's best option was to send for reinforcements.

Companon ordered de Soto and a soldier named Pedro Miguel to ride through the enemy lines. The surprise charge of two soldiers on horses galloping directly at the Indians caused a momentary break in their lines. According to one written account of the siege, the break in the lines was wide enough to "free many men."[2]

Miguel and de Soto led a small group on a one-hundred-mile journey to Panama City. They covered the distance in two days and told Pedrarias Davila about the ongoing siege. The governor initially sent 40 men as reinforcements. Then he sent 140 more soldiers. Still, the siege

continued for five days before Urraca and his men retreated.

EXPEDITION TO NICARAGUA

Although he retreated, Urraca continued to attack the Spanish invaders for another eleven years. He waged a guerrilla war against them until his death in 1531. However, the Spaniards were in the region to stay. Davila named Companon lieutenant governor and commandant of Nata. De Soto secured his reputation as a skilled soldier and a brave warrior. His actions had saved Espinosa and his army from being utterly destroyed in an ambush.

De Soto stayed in Nata until late 1523. During his time there, he amassed more plundered gold, and he captured and enslaved Indians. His future looked secure and promising. De Soto aligned himself with Companon and had a reputation as an intrepid, ruthless, and wily soldier.

In June 1523, an explorer and adventurer named Gil González Dávila arrived at Panama with three leaky ships. He came ashore with one hundred weary sailors and a reported fortune in gold worth one hundred twelve thousand pesos. González Dávila had been sent on a mission to explore the uncharted Pacific Coast of Central America. His explorations took him to a new and strange land, which he called Nicaragua.

After arriving in Panama City, González Dávila told astonishing tales about a country of great wealth. He spoke of a people ruled by powerful kings living in fancy palaces. Dávila described majestic-looking pyramids and abundant deposits of gold that were there for the taking.

Pedrarias Davila quickly heard of González Dávila's stories and lined up some investors to pay for an invasion of Nicaragua. Once the investors had raised an army, de Soto was put in command of 76 men. Sometime in late 1523, a 230-man army led by Hernandez de Cordoba sailed for the northern coast of Costa Rica, which bordered Nicaragua.

Historians know little about what occurred in the early stages of the invasion. What they do know is that the Spaniards built a fort at a place called Urutina before heading north. Historians believe that almost as soon as the Spaniards left Urutina, they faced armed attacks. De Soto was likely put in command of the invading army's lead battalion.

The Spaniards easily subdued the Nicaraguan Indians. This was a surprising feat because the Spaniards were greatly outnumbered. The Indians were armed with clubs, javelins, bows and arrows, and swords carved from stone or wood. Some also had body armor, and the highest-ranking warriors—generals and kings—wore armor made of gold.

Having more powerful and sophisticated weapons helped the Spaniards compensate for their small numbers. Their most used weapon was the saber, which had a single-edged or double-edged metal blade. Against an unarmored opponent, it was a deadly weapon. The muskets used by the Spaniards were cumbersome and inaccurate. When the soldiers fired at them, however, the fearsome noise could send an enemy running. Spanish crossbows shot arrows with enough force to pierce armor, but the weapons took a lot of time to load and fire.

The major advantage the Spaniards had was in the way the Nicaraguan Indians fought. The Indians were more interested in disabling an enemy than in killing him. Capturing prisoners was more important to them than slaying enemy soldiers. That philosophy of war doomed them to failure.

By the spring of 1524, the Spanish invaders controlled much of Nicaragua. Cordoba then turned his attention to building cities and establishing a colonial government. He founded the towns of Granada, Leon, and Segovia. Leon was named as the capital city of the new Spanish colony, and de Soto was named as one of the capital's thirty-three founding *vecinos*.

● Power Struggle

While Cordoba was using his soldiers and enslaved Indians to build his cities, other Spanish captains were coming into the area and challenging his dominance. Indian informants had told Cordoba that an expedition led by Pedro de Alvarado was in the area and headed south toward El Salvador.

Cordoba began building stockades and sending scouting parties to see if other expeditions were in on his newly claimed territory. Some of the scouts encountered an army led by González Dávila. González Dávila's army was marching south from their base in Honduras. González Dávila told the leader of the scouts that they were trespassing on his territory.

González Dávila's army was much larger than Cordoba's scouting party. The scouting party returned to Leon to tell Cordoba that González Dávila's army was approaching. About the same time, Cordoba also learned that Alvarado's army was headed their way. He sent de Soto and seventy to eighty soldiers to tell both González Dávila and Alvarado that Cordoba had already claimed Nicaragua.

In the summer of 1524, de Soto led his small army to confront Alvarado's fighting force of about five hundred men. Fortunately, de Soto's men were able to avoid fighting a much larger army. Alvarado was moving his army northward to Guatemala because the king of Mexico had appointed him as governor of that country.

That enabled de Soto to focus on finding and driving out González Dávila and his forces. In just a few days, de Soto's army traveled nearly two hundred miles in pursuit of González Dávila. When the two armies clashed, González Dávila used stealth and trickery to defeat de Soto.

González Dávila's men attacked de Soto's army while it was encamped outside of Toreba, Honduras. De Soto and his men were sleeping when the surprise attack began. Although he was taken by surprise, de Soto quickly rallied his troops. They repelled the attack, but quit fighting after González Dávila cried out to de Soto: "Senor captain! Peace, peace in the name of the king!"[3]

De Soto's own captains warned him that it was a trick, but he decided to trust González Dávila. De Soto accepted a cease-fire. After the fighting ceased, González Dávila secretly sent out for some reinforcements. That enabled him to launch a successful second surprise attack.

Dávila's forces captured de Soto but, after a brief time, González Dávila freed de Soto and his defeated army. González Dávila may have been afraid that Cordoba would send reinforcements to rout his army. Historians believe that González

Dávila kept most, if not all, of the gold that he seized from de Soto's army.

BECOMING RICH

Despite the embarrassing defeat, de Soto remained a favorite of Cordoba. The mission was still considered a success because Alvarado's and González Dávila's armies had left Nicaragua. The mission had gathered some more plundered gold. Cordoba rewarded de Soto with a share of one thousand gold pesos. De Soto also received a gift of land, shares in a gold mine, and a political appointment. At the age of twenty-four, de Soto became mayor of Leon.

Over the next several years, de Soto compiled a considerable fortune. He owned many slaves and exploited them to tend to his land and toil in the gold mines. The slave trade was yet another of his lucrative enterprises. De Soto also partnered with his friend Hernan Ponce de Leon. They bought ships and started a shipping company.

Even the accumulation of great wealth did not satisfy de Soto. He remained ambitious and restless. There were rumors that a land to the south—a place called Peru—contained a lot of gold. These rumors lured de Soto with the prospect of further adventures, conquests, and wealth. Peru would become his next destination.

Chapter 4
The Inca and the Search for Gold

After

serving together under Gaspar de Espinosa, Francisco Pizarro and Hernando de Soto had gone their separate ways. In 1522, Pizarro led a expedition that explored parts of Colombia around the San Juan River. Four years later, he led a second expedition that went into Peru and yielded a quantity of gold.

After the governor of Panama refused to sponsor any further expeditions, Pizarro traveled to Spain to appeal to King Charles V. The two agreed that Pizarro would have the right to conquer Peru for Spain and serve as its governor. In return, the king would rule all of Peru's population and claim all of the country's wealth.

However, the King did not provide funds to pay for the expedition. Pizarro raised an army by promising the recruits a percentage of the gold and any other riches they would discover. Pizarro knew that de Soto was very wealthy. He also remembered him as being a resourceful fighter and a bold leader.

⬤AN OFFER AND A BETRAYAL

Pizarro asked de Soto to join the expedition, offering to make him his second in command. But military rank was probably less important to de Soto than the allure of adventure and the prospect of more riches. De Soto sold his property, bought two ships, and raised an army of about one hundred soldiers.

In 1531, de Soto and his small army sailed off for Peru. They were accompanied by about twenty sailors, forty to fifty horses, and several hundred slaves and servants. De Soto and his men were eager to explore Peru because of the riches it offered. If they had known about the many hardships that Pizarro and his army had endured, they would not have been quite so eager.

About a year earlier, the Pizarro expedition came ashore at Puna, a small island off the coast of southwest Ecuador. Indians soon attacked the Spaniards. The Indians resented how the intruders had stolen their food and their women and seized their villages. Along with suffering casualties in sporadic skirmishes, the Spaniards were slowly starving because their food was running low.

In early December 1531, Pizarro's spirits were buoyed by the arrival of de Soto and his army. According to an account written by Pedro Pizarro, the de Soto expedition found "an island in revolt

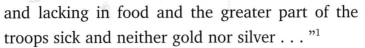

and lacking in food and the greater part of the troops sick and neither gold nor silver . . . "[1]

Along with the shock and dismay of finding a sickly, ragtag army, de Soto was upset to learn that he was not going to serve as Pizarro's second in command. Pizarro had already given that post to his brother, Hernando. De Soto's faith and confidence in Pizarro was greatly diminished if not totally shattered. From that moment on, de Soto schemed for ways to strengthen his influence and to weaken Pizarro's standing with their soldiers.

INVADING PERU

With the arrival of de Soto's reinforcements, Pizarro had an army of three hundred men—two hundred foot soldiers and one hundred horsemen—to conquer and subdue an area with about 6 million people. Early in 1532, the army departed from Puna. De Soto was the first to leave. He led a group of fifteen men on a few rafts.

De Soto was not the first to arrive in Peru. That saved his life. The three soldiers who were the first to hit the shores of Peru were quickly ambushed, tortured, and killed by the Peruvian Indians.

After the entire army landed at a town called Tumbez, the Spaniards went on the offensive. De Soto was put in charge of a vanguard of sixty-four men. The vanguard was an advance army sent to gather intelligence and scout terrain before the rest of the forces moved forward.

Before his army marched inland, Pizarro set up a coastal base. That gave him a place to dock his ships and a haven to retreat to if his army failed to fend off an attack. Once that was done, his army cautiously moved inland.

After marching for several days, Pizarro and his army reached a city called Paita. The people there surrendered to the Spaniards without even fighting. The army took their homes and food and made them their slaves. The Spaniards spent three restful months in Paita before moving on.

When they continued their march, the army followed a strict policy of not fighting unless they came under attack. Pizarro wanted to put the Peruvian Indians called the Inca at ease while he learned all he could about the size and strength of their fighting forces. His ploy worked. As his army marched through Peru, the Inca watched, but did not attack the uninvited visitors.

The Mighty Inca

The Incan empire probably started out as a small kingdom in the 1300s. In the mid-1400s, they battled to conquer their enemies and expand their empire. This began after they repelled an attack from a nearby city-state. After turning back an attacking army, the Inca went on the offensive.

By the time de Soto and Pizarro invaded Peru, the Incan empire stretched along the western coast of South America from northern Ecuador to southern Chile. That was about twenty-five hundred miles.

In late September 1532, Pizarro was impatient to attack and his army was restless. The Inca were in a weakened position because they had been fighting among themselves. Since the death of their ruler, Huayna Capac, his son, Huascar, and Atahualpa, one of the Inca's most skilled generals, were fighting to become the new ruler of the empire. Between 1528 and 1531, tens of thousands of Inca died in the power struggle.

Atahualpa prevailed after his soldiers entered the city of Cuzco, Peru, and killed almost every member of Capac's royal family. While Pizarro's army was on the march, in 1532, de Soto was leading an advance unit to a city known as Cajas. De Soto had heard that Atahualpa was resting there before he would go on to Cuzco.

THE MARCH TO CAJAMARCA

Apparently, Atahualpa was aware of de Soto's approaching army, but he did not try to ambush them. He did not think that they posed much of a threat. He was more concerned with subduing and destroying any soldiers who were still loyal to Huascar.

These are the ruins of the ancient Incan city of Machu Picchu.

When de Soto arrived in Cajas, Atahualpa was not there. De Soto told the town's leader that they were now Spanish subjects and that Atahualpa was no longer their ruler.

After leaving Cajas, de Soto and his army rejoined Pizarro's forces. An Incan ambassador traveled with them to the town of Sana. When they arrived there, the ambassador gave them gifts of gold and llamas. Pizarro told the ambassador that he wanted to meet with Atahualpa. The ambassador told Pizarro that Atahualpa would meet him in the town of Cajamarca.

As it approached Cajamarca, the invading army wondered if they were being set up for an ambush. It seemed like Atahualpa was toying with them. While the invading army slowly advanced, Atahualpa sent porters to bring them food and gifts. One of Atahualpa's spies reported to his ruler that the approaching army was nothing more than a small band of ordinary men. It was an army that the Inca could easily defeat.

On November 15, Pizarro stood on a hill overlooking Cajamarca. He was probably surprised to see a huge army encamped near the town. Reportedly, the Incan forces numbered between 40,000 and 80,000 soldiers. Pizarro's army included a mere 106 foot soldiers and 62 cavalry.

One of Pizarro's soldiers wrote about their reaction to the Inca's overwhelming numbers: "It filled all of us Spaniards with fear and confusion. But it was not appropriate to show any fear, far less to turn back."[2]

Pizarro sent some of his horsemen to find Atahualpa and arrange a meeting. De Soto was one of the horsemen chosen for the dangerous mission. They found the Incan ruler and he agreed to meet Pizarro the next day. He also allowed Pizarro's army to camp in some empty buildings around Cajamarca's town square.

TRICKING THE INCA

That evening, Pizarro and his soldiers discussed and debated their strategy. One soldier recalled: "Few slept. We kept watch in the square, from which we could see the campfires of the Indian army. It was a fearful sight."[3]

Pizarro decided that their only hope was a surprise attack. The invaders came up with a simple scheme. When Atahualpa arrived for their meeting, they would be hiding inside the buildings surrounding the square. They would invite the ruler to stay for dinner and then launch an attack before the Incan army could respond.

At around noon, the Incan army started marching in a ceremonial parade to the town square. The Incan soldiers carried no weapons. Historians believe that Atahualpa did not want to frighten the Spaniards.

A troupe of hundreds of dancers and singers accompanied the army. Incan lords and chieftains were part of the grand procession. About five or six thousand Inca crowded into the square. When Atahualpa arrived at the square, he was surprised to find there were no Spaniards waiting to receive him. He wondered if they might have fled in fear.

Suddenly a priest appeared carrying a Bible in one hand and a cross in another. He was accompanied by an Incan boy who served as his interpreter. The priest walked up to Atahualpa and began shouting a message, which the boy translated. It was a brief sermon followed by demands that the Inca recognize the king of Spain and the pope as their new masters.

Atahualpa asked the priest to hand him the Bible he had been waving. In a gesture of anger and defiance, the ruler threw it on the ground. The priest responded by giving the army a signal to attack. He shouted: "Come out, Christians! Come out at these enemy dogs who reject the things of God!"[4]

Two blasts from a cannon quickly followed those words. The Inca were stunned by the weapon's thunderous roar and the sight of several men suddenly dying. Then an army of 168 men charged out of the buildings. The unarmed Inca were crammed into an area with no escape route. Sharpened swords and heavy lances cut through them as they tried to flee. They fell over one another, and one eyewitness reported that the fallen Inca "formed mounds and suffocated one another."[5]

The massacre continued for about two hours. Historians estimate that during that time each Spanish soldier killed an average of fifteen Inca. Eyewitness accounts estimated that the Spaniards slaughtered between two thousand and eight thousand Inca. Pizarro's army had no reported deaths. Their only reported casualty was Pizarro receiving a small cut on his hand.

The Spaniards captured Atahualpa, but spared his life. That evening he dined with Pizarro while de Soto and other horsemen continued to hunt down and kill unarmed, fleeing Inca. The killing finally ended after the blaring of bugles summoned the horsemen back to their encampment.

A Room Filled With Gold

Shortly after his capture, Atahualpa bargained for his freedom. He had noticed how strongly the invaders were attracted to the precious metals of the Inca. He met with Pizarro and made an unbelievable offer. Atahualpa took a piece of chalk and drew a line as high he could reach on the room's wall. Then he offered to fill the room with treasure up to the chalk line.

The room would be filled three times—once with gold and twice with silver. There are estimates claiming that the treasure room was 17 by 22 feet. That would have been 374 square feet of gold and 748 square feet of silver. It would truly be a king's ransom.

The generosity of the offer amazed Pizarro. He ordered his secretary to write down the terms of the offer and then had Atahualpa sign the paper. After the signing, Pizarro had de Soto and some other senior staff members witness the Incan chief pledge to honor their agreement.

While the ransom was being gathered, Atahualpa was allowed to rule his conquered people. He still issued orders and met with his advisers. That kept the remains of the Incan empire functioning and maintained the peace between the Inca and the Spaniards.

It took several months for such a vast quantity of gold and silver to be transported to Cajamarca. The precious metals arrived in the form of cups, plates, statues, building tiles, and jewelry. Then the objects were melted down and molded into small bars. According to Pizarro's secretary, more than eleven tons of gold were melted down. The silver objects produced thirteen tons of silver bars. An estimate made in 1995 placed the value of the ransom at $91 million. The ransom would probably be worth more than $100 million today.

🌑 BETRAYING THE INCA

De Soto reportedly received 31,080 gold pesos and 1,267 silver marks as his share of the ransom. Once the ransom was divided among the soldiers, few still cared about freeing Atahualpa or sparing his life. De Soto argued that they should not execute someone who had made them wealthy by honoring an agreement.

Pizarro disagreed, but he did not act until after he got de Soto to leave Cajamarca. He told de Soto that there were rumors of an impending Incan attack in an area called Ruminavi. Pizarro sent de Soto to see if there were any troops coming from that area.

While de Soto was away, Pizarro swiftly put Atahualpa on trial and sentenced the Incan ruler to die. Pizarro could have delayed the trial until de Soto's return, but he wanted to act quickly. The Spaniards executed Atahualpa by garroting. A wet leather strap was tightly placed around his neck. As the strap dried out, it began shrinking. The shrinking strap slowly and painfully strangled the Incan ruler.

When Spanish king, Charles V, learned of the execution, he sent a letter to Pizarro that expressed his strong displeasure: "We have been displeased by the death of Atahualpa, since he was a monarch and particularly as it was done in the name of justice."[6]

De Soto reportedly had an angry confrontation with Pizarro after hearing the news of Atahualpa's execution. He told Pizarro that he was leaving Peru and returning to Spain. But de Soto soon found out that leaving was not possible. The Inca were fighting back and they had to be subdued.

In an eight-hundred-mile march from Cajamarca to the Incan capital of Cuzco, Pizarro's army fought four major battles with the Inca. The Inca fought bravely, but they were waging war with maces, darts, and slingshots. The Spaniards had razor-sharp steel swords, daggers, and lances.

Some of Pizzaro's soldiers also had the advantage of being on horseback. That gave them greater speed, height, and mobility. A mounted soldier could use his horse to run down an enemy while slashing his weapon downward. Historians estimate that for every Spaniard killed, hundreds of Inca were slain.

ROBBERY ON A GRAND SCALE

On November 15, 1533, Pizarro's victorious army marched into Cuzco. Seizing all the treasures in the conquered capital was a top priority. They took every available bit of gold and silver and melted it down. The total value of the treasure was even greater than that of Atahualpa's ransom.

A priest who witnessed the unrestrained looting wrote that the only concern of Pizarro's army

The Spaniards executed Atahualpa, the last Inca King of Peru, on August 29, 1533.

was ". . . to collect gold and silver to make themselves all rich . . . without thinking that they were doing wrong and were wrecking and destroying. For what was being destroyed was more perfect than anything they enjoyed and possessed."[7]

After helping Pizarro complete his conquest, de Soto stayed in Peru until 1535. He served as lieutenant governor of Cuzco and gathered even greater wealth. When he left Peru, de Soto filled a ship with his many possessions—furniture, slaves, Incan treasures, and, of course, bars of silver and gold. He would return to Spain respected, if not revered, as a fierce and brave soldier who had slain hundreds of Inca and gained a large fortune while doing it.

But in spite of his great fame, glory, and wealth, de Soto remained unfulfilled. He yearned for further conquests and adventures. He would find them after winning the approval of King Charles V.

Chapter 5

Journeying Through Florida

In the spring of 1536, Hernando de Soto returned to Spain and docked his ship, the Santa Maria del Campo, at the port of Seville. When he left the country around 1514, he had been an unknown poor mercenary seeking his fortune in the New World. Now he was returning as a conquering hero bringing back a personal fortune of one thousand pounds of gold.

Within a few weeks, de Soto bought a home befitting a man of his wealth and status. His new home was an enormous palace with a large courtyard and servants to tend the estate. But at the age of thirty-six, de Soto was not ready to settle down to the quiet life of a wealthy retired soldier and explorer.

PLANNING FOR FLORIDA

Since his return to Spain, de Soto had heard tales from old friends about a vast unexplored territory called Florida. A few bold Spanish explorers had briefly set foot on Florida's southern coast, but American Indians and dense forests kept them from venturing very far inland. De Soto wondered if this unexplored territory could offer even more gold and other riches than Peru had yielded.

In the spring of 1537, de Soto met with King Charles V. There is no record of their encounter, but shortly after they met, the king informally granted de Soto permission to explore and invade Florida.

De Soto would not be the first to explore and try to claim Florida for Spain. Ponce de León had made two attempts. The first attempt, in 1513, ended after his expedition was attacked by Calusa Indians. The second attempt, in 1519, ended after Ponce de León was killed in another Indian skirmish near Charlotte Harbor.

On April 20, 1537, de Soto and Charles V signed an agreement that gave de Soto the right to conquer and settle Florida. Before the signing, lawyers for both sides settled the questions of how much tax de Soto would have to pay on the gold he mined or plundered and how many years he would have to complete his mission.

The agreement also required de Soto to take a minimum of five hundred men, including Catholic priests to convert American Indians to join their faith. The agreement further said that de Soto, not the Spanish government, would pay for the undertaking. In return, the King appointed de Soto as the governor of Cuba.

De Soto had no trouble recruiting soldiers for the new expedition. Between January and March 1538, about seven hundred men signed up for the expedition. Along with soldiers, de Soto also recruited blacksmiths, sailors, carpenters, and medical staff. He purchased at least five large ships and three or more smaller vessels for the expedition. A crew of about 130 sailors would man and maintain the fleet.

TRAINING IN CUBA

It took nearly a year to fully equip the expedition. On April 7, 1538, de Soto's fleet departed Sanlucar, Spain, and sailed into the North Atlantic Ocean. They were accompanied by an additional fleet of twenty large ships on its way back to Mexico. After about two months, the fleets separated. The Mexican fleet sailed on to Veracruz, Mexico, and de Soto's ships continued on to Cuba.

Once he settled in Cuba, de Soto set up the colonial government and established himself as governor. He also trained his army and bought more horses and supplies for his soldiers. By early autumn, de Soto handpicked a unit of 150 cavalrymen to go with him on a 450-mile march from Santiago, Cuba, to Havana.

The long march gave de Soto an opportunity to check how well the government was working in the towns and districts he visited. He was also able to buy more horses and supplies. Most important, the long march enabled de Soto to train and prepare the mounted soldiers that would become the core of his army during the Florida expedition.

During the march, de Soto exploited the resources of every town and settlement he visited.

He demanded that the townspeople feed and house his soldiers at their expense. De Soto treated the Spanish settlers as coldly and callously as he had treated the Inca in Peru. Since the Spanish settlers did not offer any armed resistance, they avoided bloodshed.

After reaching Havana, de Soto finalized the plans and preparations for his Florida expedition. He and his wife, Isabel, moved into a spacious house, and de Soto decreed that she would serve as acting governor while he was away. Sometime in late 1538, de Soto told Juan de Anasco to take two small ships and a fifty-man crew to Florida. De Soto instructed de Anasco to find a suitable harbor for de Soto's army to land.

When de Anasco returned to Cuba, he met de Soto with some incredible news. While he was in Florida, de Anasco had captured four Timucuan. He brought them back with him to meet de Soto.

Hernando de Soto's Florida expedition left from San Lucar, Spain, on April 7, 1538.

Using sign language, the captives told de Soto "... much gold exists in Florida."[1]

De Soto was happy to hear the news, even though it came from a doubtful source. The captives had no proof to verify their claim. Nor had de Anasco asked them to show him where the gold was located. Yet, their claim probably convinced de Soto that vast riches exceeding even the Incan treasures were waiting for him in Florida.

Sometime in mid-May 1539, de Soto signed his will and prepared for his next great adventure. On May 18, a fleet of nine ships sailed out of Havana. On board were about 600 soldiers, 130 sailors, and an unknown number of slaves and servants. There were also around 240 horses for the cavalry and an unknown number of packhorses and mules that would carry supplies.

First Impressions

De Soto and his fleet landed in Florida in late May. Historians still dispute exactly where they landed. It may have been in Tampa Bay or at Charlotte Harbor, which is seventy-five miles south of Tampa Bay. Some scholars and historians believe that the correct site was San Carlos Bay, fifteen miles south of Charlotte Harbor.

Wherever he landed, de Soto quickly took charge. He had his men clear out land for a campsite. They cleared underbrush, chopped down

De Soto says goodbye to his wife, Isabel, in Havana, Cuba, in 1539 before sailing for Florida. Isabel would serve as governor of Cuba in the explorer's absence.

trees, and began unloading the ships. De Soto also sent a small scouting party to keep an eye out for American Indians.

The first time a scouting party ventured forth they skirmished with some Indians. Two Indians were killed and two horses were wounded before the other Indians escaped into the dense and swampy woods.

As de Soto's expedition moved slowly northward, it traveled in three separate units. A

Two re-enactors fire a salute shot near the De Soto National Memorial in Bradenton, Florida. Historians believe this is near the site where de Soto landed in 1539.

vanguard led the way. It was composed of mostly horsemen, but occasionally a few foot soldiers would travel with them. The vanguard would clear a path for the rest of the expedition to follow.

The vanguard was followed by the majority of the expedition. It had most of the army's foot soldiers and a few horsemen. Porters, servants, slaves, and the few women in the expedition were in this group. The animals that de Soto brought along—pigs, horses, and dogs—were also a part of the group.

A rear guard trailed behind the main body. It consisted of a few horsemen to protect the main body from being attacked.

As his army marched northward, de Soto sent scouting parties to explore the terrain and look for food. He kept his army fed by moving from village to village and taking whatever food the Indians had stored. De Soto's army also captured anyone who could be useful as a guide or porter.

A Fortunate Discovery

In early June 1539, the expedition reached an abandoned Indian town named Ocita. De Soto made that his base of operations for about the next six weeks. De Soto had wanted to capture some Indians to serve as translators and guides. But that was proving to be a difficult task. The Indians easily escaped into the swamps and forests. One group in particular, the Timucuan, were very skilled warriors.

The Timucuan used a weapon called a long-bow. It was called that because it was about six to seven feet long. In the hands of a skilled archer, the longbow could accurately shoot an arrow up to two hundred paces. The sharpened arrowheads

could pierce the protective iron mail worn by the Spanish soldiers.

On the morning of July 15, 1539, de Soto left Ocita and resumed his northward journey. During his encampment in Ocita, de Soto had been able to find a translator and a trail guide that he had sought. Juan Ortiz was a Spaniard who had been

This nineteenth-century engraving shows the expedition of Hernando de Soto at Tampa Bay, Florida, in 1539.

living with the Indians in Florida for around ten years. He had been captured by the Indians during a previous Spanish expedition. Ortiz joined the expedition after some of de Soto's soldiers found him living among the Indians.

Although Ortiz is credited with helping to make peace between the Spaniards and the Indians, there were still occasional attacks and skirmishes. De Soto's soldiers soon learned to

De Soto's soldiers found Juan Ortiz, a Spanish captive and survivor of the Narváez expedition of 1528, living with Florida Indians in 1539. Ortiz would serve with de Soto's expedition. This 1904 illustration shows de Soto saving Ortiz.

march in a close formation because stragglers became easy prey for the Indians.

The northern journey proceeded slowly. Many rivers, wetlands, and marshes slowed the army's progress. Sometimes the march came to a complete stop until de Soto's soldiers built a bridge across a river.

AMBUSH!

On July 26, de Soto and the vanguard reached the Ocale Indians. Today, that area is known as Ocala, Florida. At that time, Ocala was a mere village. The Ocale had been anticipating de Soto's arrival and had left the village. There were only empty houses made out of palm thatches by the time de Soto arrived.

There was no gold to be found in Ocala, but there was a lot of corn, along with pumpkins, plums, and other fruits. De Soto and his army camped there to rest from days of marching in the hot, humid weather. While his men rested and regained their strength, de Soto probably pondered his situation. After two months of marching and exploring, they had found no gold and had lost several soldiers and horses during surprise attacks.

If de Soto was bothered by any self-doubts, he did not let it show. After a few days of resting, de Soto received a surprise visitor—the chief of the

Ocale. De Soto greeted him and asked the chief to loan him some of his warriors to help them build a bridge. The chief agreed.

When de Soto accompanied the chief to inspect the proposed construction site, some two hundred Ocale sprang out of the nearby thickets. They launched a volley of arrows at de Soto, but his armor and helmet protected him. Historians do not known exactly how many soldiers de Soto had with him, but his army rebuffed the surprise attack. The chief claimed that he was not responsible for the attack because his warriors had disobeyed him.

Apparently, the bridge was built without any assistance from the Ocale. The Spaniards then resumed their northern trek. Their next destination was a place called Apalachee. There were no reports of gold in that particular area. Historians believe that de Soto came there to find food for the upcoming winter. He also wanted to conquer and subdue the Apalachee Indians who had chased away an earlier Spanish explorer named Pánfilo de Narváez.

A Kidnapping

One day after crossing the river, one of de Soto's scouting parties captured a group of seventeen Indians. One of the captives was the daughter of a chief named Aguacaleyquen. That same day, the chief greeted de Soto when his army moved into the capital of the king's domain, which was also called Aguacaleyquen. The Spaniards took the chief hostage after he offered to exchange himself for his daughter's freedom.

On August 22, a "great multitude of Indians"[2] descended on de Soto's camp. They believed that a show of force would scare de Soto into releasing

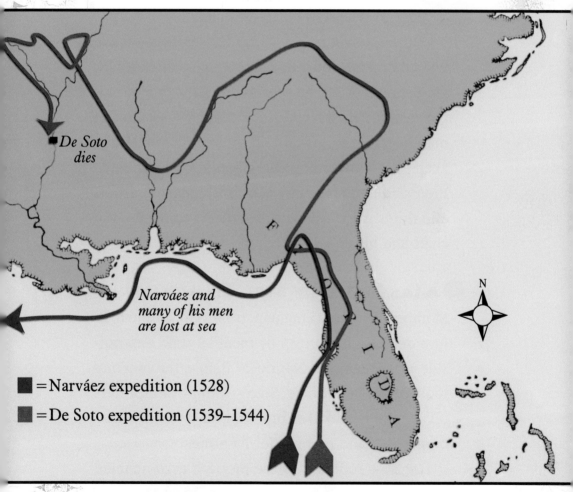

■ De Soto dies

Narváez and many of his men are lost at sea

■ = Narváez expedition (1528)

■ = De Soto expedition (1539–1544)

N

This map shows the routes taken by de Soto and Narváez through the American Southeast.

the chief and his daughter. It had the opposite effect. De Soto put his camp on full alert and sent for reinforcements to aid the threatened vanguard.

The Indians refrained from attacking. But they still monitored the Spanish army's movements. As the army marched on, allies of Aguacaleyqguen gathered around them and repeatedly asked for de Soto to release the captive chief.

On September 9, de Soto left Aguacaleyquen with the chief and his daughter still in captivity. On September 15, he reached the next major city, which was called Napituca. During the six days of marching, large groups of Indians continued to keep a watchful eye on the Spaniards. They made the invaders nervous by constantly playing drums and flutes while asking the invaders to release the chief and his daughter.

MASSACRE OF THE TIMUCUAN

Members of the Timucuan tribe had planned to lure de Soto into a trap by meeting with him outside of his camp at Napituca. Before the meeting took place, one of de Soto's Indian interpreters revealed the plan. De Soto ordered his men to arm themselves and prepare for an attack.

De Soto rode out to the meeting accompanied by a small guard. Almost as soon as de Soto and his guard arrived at the meeting place, Timucuan warriors armed with bows and arrows surrounded them. De Soto was ready for the ambush. He ordered his trumpeter to blow his horn loudly. That was the signal for the Spaniards to attack.

Although the Timucuan were taken by surprise, they reportedly fought "like men of great spirit"[3] and for "a good period of time."[4] They killed a horse that de Soto was riding. They also killed several other horses and soldiers before being defeated.

The battle was fought in a flat clearing. The Timucuan could not hide behind trees or in foliage. The mounted Spanish soldiers had no trouble running the Timucuan down and then hacking them to death with their lances and swords. The Timucuan retreated into two small nearby ponds. They were trapped in the frigid waters. When they emerged from the ponds, the Spaniards tied them up and marched them back to their camp.

The imprisoned warriors were forced to perform degrading menial tasks, which they strongly resented. They had to carry equipment, tend the horses, and do anything else their captors ordered. At one point, the resentment turned to open defiance.

When the Spaniards released one Timucuan chief from his chains, he punched de Soto in the mouth. De Soto spit blood, and a full-scale uprising quickly ensued. Some of the Timucuan seized lances and swords that the Spaniards had carelessly left out. But most of the captives were still bound by ropes or chains.

Within a few minutes, the Spaniards had regained the upper hand. An enraged de Soto executed most of the survivors. The youngest boys were spared so they could be trained to become servants. The rest of the defiant Timucuan were tied to a stake and killed by a firing squad. The squad was composed of Indian collaborators armed with bows and arrows.

De Soto's behavior puzzles some historians. At that time, he needed servants to aid his army, but he chose to kill about two hundred men who could have served him. Even some of de Soto's soldiers found the punishment excessive and foolish. They thought the execution of only a few Indians would have sent the same message.

More Kidnappings

One week after the mass executions, de Soto and his army continued north. After marching about ten miles, they came upon a large river, which is believed to be the Suwannee River in northern Florida. They stopped to build a bridge. That project delayed their progress for a few days.

After crossing the river they camped first in the village of Uzachile, and then in the village of

Aucilla. Both villages were deserted. The chiefs had been warned of the army's impending arrival, and they had learned about the massacre at Napituca. They had decided that it was better to flee than to fight.

While encamped in Uzachile, de Soto sent two of his captains to search the surrounding area for Indians. They captured about one hundred. De Soto took two of the women captives as his personal servants and perhaps as mistresses. The Spaniards chained up the remaining captives with collars and forced them to perform menial tasks.

By the end of September 1539, the army was entering the domain of the Apalachee. The Apalachee were a tribe with a reputation for being fierce warriors. In 1528, the Spanish explorer and soldier, Pánfilo de Narváez and his army entered their territory in search of gold. Narváez and his men disappeared.

De Soto knew of Narváez's ill-fated expedition, but he was undaunted. Even though it meant facing his first serious military challenge, de Soto was determined to conquer the Apalachee.

Chapter 6

Lost!

AS Hernando de Soto's army moved on, their Timucuan guides pleaded with them to turn back. They told tales of the Apalachee's bravery in battle and their cruelty toward conquered foes. Some of de Soto's soldiers were certainly weary and fearful. For four months they had endured almost constant Indian attacks, unrelenting heat and humidity, and swampy, unfamiliar terrain.

In return for their efforts, they had found no gold and were now facing the prospect of fighting a determined and disciplined enemy.

Encountering the Apalachee

The Apalachee leadership was well aware that the Spaniards were on the march. Their scouts had been monitoring the movements of de Soto's army. A large force of warriors, numbering in the hundreds, if not the thousands, was preparing to defend the eastern border of their territory.

Although the Apalachee were without horses, their encounter with Narváez had given them experience with fighting the Spanish cavalrymen. It had also given them knowledge of Spanish weapons, battle tactics, and armor. They felt that they had little to fear.

On October 1, de Soto had his first skirmish with the Apalachee. On that day, he had reached a forest bordering the Aucilla River in northern Florida. The Apalachee quickly attacked de Soto's

vanguard unit. Since the river was at flood stage, the movement of de Soto's army was hampered.

De Soto gathered a force to attack and repel the Apalachee. They marched into waist-high water and spent most of the day fighting. The Spanish gained the advantage after they fought their way out of the water and into open fields.

One account claims that after the Apalachee had been forced out, the Spaniards "did not meet a single Indian whom they failed to capture or kill."[1]

After repelling the attack, the army marched on to the town of Ivitachuco, a few miles up the flooded river. The Apalachee had anticipated their arrival and had set the town on fire. The Spaniards arrived in time to keep the crops from burning. They picked as much corn and other vegetables as they could carry. After the fire burned itself out, they set up camp in the town.

The Apalachee had the military advantage over the Spaniards when it came to fighting on water.

The Spaniards rested for one day before resuming their march north to the Apalachee's capital city of Anhaica. During the march, hostile guides futilely tried to mislead de Soto and his army. The Spaniards also endured some sporadic hit-and-run attacks from the Apalachee along the way.

ENDURING APALACHEE RAIDS

Historians believe that the Apalachee capital was deserted when de Soto got there. In their haste to leave, the Apalachee departed without setting it on fire. De Soto settled into the abandoned capital and turned it into a fortress for his army. He also sent out messengers to find the king of the Apalachee and ask for his surrender.

Rather than surrender, the Apalachee continued their practice of raids and hit-and-run attacks against the Spaniards. When the Spaniards were out gathering food, Apalachee archers would attack them. Still, de Soto would boldly send out squadrons of soldiers to survey and explore the surrounding region. Eventually, he decided that the best way to protect his men would be by attacking the Apalachee.

De Soto sent Juan de Anasco, one of his most able and trusted captains, back to Ocita for reinforcements. De Anasco took thirty of de Soto's best horsemen with him. They knew that they would succeed only if they moved swiftly through the hostile territory. In only ten days, de Anasco completed a journey that had taken de Soto's army eleven weeks.

During the perilous journey, they survived several Indian attacks while crossing swamps and rivers. They only lost two soldiers along the way. Both of them died from unknown illnesses.

While de Anasco was away, de Soto used extreme measures in trying to frighten the Apalachee into surrender and submission. He tortured them by cutting off their noses and hands or by burning them at the stake. The Apalachee retaliated by launching major attacks upon their heavily fortified former capital. They tossed torches and shot flaming arrows over the walls of the town. The Apalachee also continued to ambush Spanish soldiers when they were out picking fruit or gathering food.

Historians believe that the Apalachee killed around twenty Spaniards during the five months that they were encamped at Anhanica. Still, the Apalachee suffered much greater casualties. De Soto became more frustrated by the resistance of the Apalachee, but the hope of finding great riches kept him from retreating. This hope was buoyed by the tales told by a teenage Indian boy who had been captured by de Soto's soldiers.

⚫ LEAVING THE APALACHEE

The soldiers nicknamed the boy Perico. Perico transfixed the soldiers with fanciful tales about a kingdom that had been his home. A powerful queen ruled the kingdom and regularly collected vast amounts of gold and silver from Indian chiefs paying her tribute.

De Soto had doubts about Perico's tales until the boy described how gold was mined, melted down, and then refined. Perico told his captors that this wealthy kingdom was only a twelve- or thirteen-day march away. When de Soto heard these tales, it was likely that he had already planned to spend the winter at Anhanica. But when spring arrived, he continued the quest for the riches that had eluded him. He made plans to have supplies shipped from Cuba.

De Soto sent Francisco Maldonado to find a suitable port for the supply ships. After doing some scouting and exploring, Maldonado reported the discovery of a large bay to the west which he called Achuse. It was a sheltered port with deep enough water for the supply ships to drop anchor. Maldonado had found either Florida's Pensacola Bay or Mobile Bay in Alabama.

Shortly after returning to Anhanica, Maldonado was sent on another mission. This time de Soto ordered him to return to Cuba with letters detailing the plans to find a golden kingdom. He also ordered Maldonado to organize a fleet of supply ships to meet him and his army in Achuse the following fall.

On March 3, 1540, de Soto led his army out of Anhanica. The ranks of his expedition had been greatly diminished by the deaths of several hundred Indian slaves during the winter months. They had been forced to sleep on the cold, damp ground while being weighed down by heavy iron chains. De Soto had provided them little food, shelter, or clothing. He had long regarded slaves as being expendable and easily replaced commodities.

The Apalachee were glad to see the invaders leave. They allowed the Spaniards to march northward without attacking them. They probably believed that they had finally run them off of their land.

The deaths of so many slaves placed an extra burden on de Soto's army. Along with their weapons and supplies, the soldiers had to carry their own food rations.

An Unsure Guide

Perico was guiding the expedition. After about two days of marching, Perico led the army into their first major obstacle. The Flint River in what is now southern Georgia was swollen from the runoff of

Hernando de Soto, wearing his armor, meets with an American Indian chief. The Spanish explorer had rocky relations with many American Indian groups, mostly because he treated them very poorly.

melted snow. De Soto ordered his men to build a large canoe to cross the river.

Once the canoe had crossed the swollen waters, the Spaniards took the chains that once held their Indian slaves and joined them into one long chain to reach across the river. Then, soldiers used the chain to pull the canoe across the water. It took four days to get all the men and supplies to the other bank of the Flint River.

On March 11, the army entered an abandoned village called Capachequi. There were only a few empty huts, but there was an ample supply of food. The Spaniards took all they could before resuming their march.

During their time in Georgia, de Soto's army was usually treated well by their American Indian hosts. The Indians provided the Spaniards with food and men to help the army carry their supplies. One local king named Patofa even accompanied them on their march. They were friendly because the army was going to confront the Cofitachequi, a longtime enemy of other Indian groups in Georgia.

The friendly Indians told the Spaniards fascinating stories about the Cofitachequi. They spoke of their warriors' ferocity and determination in battle. They mentioned that the Cofitachequi were rumored to live in large cities teeming with gold.

LOST IN THE WILDERNESS

De Soto's army had reached the northern edge of Georgia's Indian kingdoms. De Soto was having major doubts about Perico's ability to lead them to the fabled golden cities. He finally confronted their guide and asked him how much farther it was to the home of the Cofitachequi. Perico was too intimidated to say that he did not know. He stalled for more time by telling de Soto it was four days away.

As usual, the lure of gold and great riches urged de Soto on. Even if Perico was lying or just misinformed, he was valuable to de Soto's expedition. His ability to communicate with various Indian groups had made him indispensable.

After Perico's predicted four-day march had stretched into nine days, the Spaniards' halted their advance by a large river. They had probably encountered the Savannah River, which runs through east Gerogia. De Soto could no longer tolerate Perico's deceptions. He confronted him, and Perico admitted that he was lost. He begged for de Soto to spare his life.

De Soto let him live because of his language skills. However, the Spaniards placed Perico in chains for the remainder of the expedition. The following day, de Soto met with his key advisers and officers to discuss their options. A few men were bold enough to suggest turning back, but de Soto quickly rejected that idea. He always believed that it was better to go forward.

Since food was running low, de Soto told Patofa and his men to return home. The Spaniards no longer had enough food to feed them. De Soto increased the food rations by slaughtering some of the pigs that had been brought along. Each man now got a daily ration of half a pound of meat.

Some of de Soto's soldiers were beginning to covet food more than gold. Still, they pressed on in search of Cofitachequi. They crossed into present-day South Carolina where de Soto finally encountered the queen of Cofitachequi on May 1, 1540. After de Soto assured her that they came in peace, the queen warmly received the Spaniards.

A WEALTH OF PEARLS

During de Soto's stay in Cofitachequi, the queen told him she would bring him the yellow and white precious metals he wanted. It would just take a few days to transport them. De Soto's excitement turned to disappointment when he was given samples of copper and mica instead of gold and silver.

Yet, the Spaniards did find some treasure to plunder. Cofitachequi was rich in pearls. The queen presented de Soto with several basketfuls of the coveted gems. De Soto also helped himself

The queen of Cofitachequi shows de Soto her vast supply of pearls and other valuable stones.

to a large quantity of pearls housed in Indian temples.

A lot, if not most, of de Soto's men would have been happy to stay in Cofitachequi. They were getting enough to eat and were enjoying their host's gracious hospitality. De Soto refused to stay. Since there was no gold there, he saw no reason to stay. He had heard of another land with an abundance of gold. It was called Chiaha.

DE SOTO TAKES MORE SLAVES

On May 13, de Soto's army was on the march again. They headed northwest into present-day North Carolina. They hiked into the territory of the Cherokee Indians, who were friendly and welcoming. The Cherokee shared their food and helped the army carry their supplies. Thanks to their help, de Soto's army became the first Europeans to cross the Appalachian Mountains. On May 31, they reached Chiaha, about twenty-five miles east of present-day Knoxville, Tennessee.

Chiaha had ample food, but no gold. That was a relief to the soldiers, but it was another disappointment for de Soto. The Indians were gracious hosts, but after about three weeks, de Soto turned on them. He began acting like a dictator instead of a welcomed guest. De Soto demanded that his hosts give him thirty of their women.

The Indians did not respond with violence. They knew that force would be met with greater force and brutality. Instead, during the early hours of June 20, the residents of Chiaha quietly deserted their capital. They vainly hoped that the Spaniards would leave them alone. Their actions infuriated de Soto. He led a group of soldiers to hunt them down and destroy their cornfields. But when he found his prey, he did not attack them. Instead, he worked out a compromise.

If the Indians would serve de Soto's army as porters, he would drop his demand for their women. They agreed to his terms. About five hundred Indians served as porters.

🌐 MAKING ENEMIES

Sometime in early July, the expedition reached Coosa. Historians still dispute the exact location of that settlement. It was either in present-day Alabama or Georgia. This area was occupied and controlled by the Creek Indians. Although the Creek were not hostile or aggressive, de Soto captured their chief to ensure the safety of his expedition.

While in Coosa, de Soto and his army continued their cruel and arrogant behavior toward Indians who had greeted them warmly. After capturing their chief, they made demands for women, food, and servants. When the Indians ran away, de Soto sent his soldiers to hunt them down and have them killed or enslaved.

This despicable behavior had been going on for so long that word of it had probably reached an Indian chief known as Tascalusa. His tribe was the Atahachi. At a place called Mabila, they would engage de Soto and his army in the bloodiest and fiercest fighting they would experience.

Chapter 7

The Mighty Mississippi

On August 20, 1540, with a fresh supply of Indian slaves swelling their numbers, the Spaniards left Coosa. About one month later, they reached Talisi. The town was abandoned when they arrived. While staying in Talisi, de Soto released the chief of the Coosa, but he refused to release his sister.

A Great Chief Captured

It was also in Talisi that de Soto first met some representatives who were sent by Tascalusa to greet him. De Soto had heard stories about the Atahachi's military might and their fierceness in battle. After the meeting, de Soto sent two men to travel with the Atahachi representatives. Their presumed mission was to spy on the Atahachi and report back to de Soto. There were rumors that a surprise attack was imminent.

At that time, de Soto was probably more concerned about meeting Maldonado and his fleet of supply ships than in fending off a surprise attack. Tascalusa's son was guiding their movements from Talisi to the capital of the Atahachi (also called Atahachi). On October 10, de Soto and Tascalusa finally met.

According to most accounts, Tascalusa greeted de Soto with an almost haughty disdain. In spite of the chief's cold greeting, the Atahachi entertained the Spaniards with a large feast and an evening of entertainment. But when the festivities ended, de Soto began issuing his usual demands—women to serve his soldiers and men to carry their supplies.

Tascalusa responded in a manner befitting his position of authority. He told de Soto that he "was not wont to serve anyone, rather that all everyone served him."[1]

De Soto had Tascalusa arrested and placed under armed guards. The following day, Tascalusa appeared to submit to de Soto. He provided the explorer with four hundred Indian men to serve as porters, but he held off on supplying his captors with food and women.

Tascalusa told de Soto that when his army reached Mabila he would provide them with ample food and one hundred of his most desirable women. For the next six days, the army marched along the banks of the Alabama River. During that march, a band of local Indians killed two Spaniards. De Soto threatened to torture Tascalusa if the chief did not give him the Indians who killed the two men.

☉ INCREASING TENSION

Although he was a prisoner, Tascalusa refused to be intimidated. He told de Soto that he would turn over the culprits when they reached Mabila. Tascalusa had already issued orders for all of his available warriors to gather in Mabila and prepare for battle.

De Soto became more suspicious of the captive chief. He sent two scouts to explore the route leading to Mabila. On October 16, one of the scouts reported back to de Soto. He informed him that many armed warriors had entered the settlement and it looked like they were preparing for a major battle.

Against the advice of some senior officers, de Soto continued on to Mabila. Once again, de Soto was convinced that he knew what was best for his army. As usual, he thought that cautious behavior was cowardly. On the morning of October 18, de Soto briefly paused before riding into the walled city of Mabila.

He was warmly received by the local chief who gave him some fur blankets as a welcoming gift. The Indians served a sumptuous feast to de Soto, and some graceful women dancers entertained him. But while de Soto was enjoying himself, Tascalusa had slipped away to confer with some of his aides.

De Soto had led a vanguard unit into the plaza of the walled city. Tascalusa and his aides discussed whether they should slaughter the advance unit at once, or wait for the rest of the army to arrive. Tascalusa and his aides decided that it would be best to attack at once.

A Bloody Battle

According to eyewitness accounts, de Soto noticed that Tascalusa had slipped away. He located the house where Tascalusa was hiding and asked him to come out. Tascalusa refused, and de Soto's men then noticed that the houses inside the walled city were not empty. They were full of armed warriors.

The first blood was shed when one of de Soto's soldiers drew his sword and severed the arm of a warrior. Moments later, thousands of Indians armed with bows, maces, and clubs stormed out of the houses and huts inside the plaza. Various accounts say that Tascalusa's army numbered from three thousand to eleven thousand men.

During the first few minutes of the surprise attack, five Spaniards were slain by arrows and maces. De Soto sustained numerous hits from arrows, but none of them penetrated his armor. He managed to mount a horse and charge into his attackers to clear a path for his soldiers. De Soto and his surviving soldiers were able to escape through the walled city's main gate.

Hernando de Soto and members of his expedition fight against Indian warriors under Chief Tuscalusa at the Battle of Mauvila (or Mabila) in what is now present-day Alabama, October 1540.

After retreating, de Soto regrouped his forces. He organized his men into four squadrons to attack the walled city on all four sides. They repeatedly charged the walls and hacked at them with axes and swords. While they attacked, reinforcements arrived. Sometime in the late afternoon, the Spaniards broke through a wall and began burning the city's thatch-roofed houses.

Hundreds of Atahachi became trapped inside the walls. They were burned to death or probably perished from smoke inhalation. Those who could escape were massacred by the waiting soldiers. Other Atahachi opted to commit suicide by running into the burning houses.

The carnage ceased around sunset. There are no accurate estimates of the total casualties. The estimated number of Indians killed ranges from 2,500 to 11,000. The Spaniards lost about 22 men and 80 horses. They also had between 150 and 250 wounded.

De Soto's forces suffered in other ways beyond the loss of life. The raging fire destroyed most of their supplies and their cache of plundered pearls. What little treasure they had taken was now gone. The sagging morale of the soldiers who had faithfully and obediently served de Soto was nearing its lowest point. The ragged and battered army was dazed and again doubting de Soto's leadership and judgment.

But the losses for the Atahachi were even more devastating. Virtually every male in that region who was capable of fighting was killed or wounded. The battle effectively ended a civilization that had taken the Atahachi centuries to create.

⬤A New Challenge

De Soto's soldiers spent the next three to four weeks tending to their wounded and searching for more food. Historians believe that between thirteen and thirty-five Spanish soldiers died from lingering wounds shortly after the battle. That means about one out of every fourteen soldiers in de Soto's army died in the battle of Mabila.

Sometime around mid-November, the remains of de Soto's army resumed their expedition. Some soldiers were now wearing blankets and sandals made of bark. Almost all of their spare clothes had been lost in the fire at Mabila. The army took a northwesterly route into what is now the state of Mississippi. Along the way, they foraged for food and built bonfires at night to warm them from the snow and cold rain.

Historians do not know why de Soto did not lead his army to Maldonado's waiting supply ships in Achusi. De Soto's army was in dire need of food, clothes, medicine, and other supplies. The waiting ships could have taken them back to Cuba. De Soto refused to accept failure. His concern for saving his reputation was greater than his concern for saving his army. Returning to Cuba without any treasure would be admitting that his mission had failed.

The weary army and their beleaguered leader encamped for the winter in an abandoned town in the Chicasa territory in northeastern Mississippi. The Chicasa had left after learning of the army's impending arrival. There was enough corn in their fields to keep de Soto's army from starving.

In January 1541, a Chicasa chief and a few tribal officials visited de Soto's camp. They brought gifts of blankets, furs, and rabbits to try to gain de Soto's trust. For several weeks they maintained friendly relations, but de Soto remained suspicious and distrustful.

During the early hours of March 4, a war party of about three hundred Chicasa launched a surprise attack upon the slumbering Spanish army. It began with some warriors setting fire to the straw roofs of huts. According to an eyewitness account, "they caught fire immediately in the hard wind that was blowing."[2]

The fiery attack was accompanied by loud battle cries and the beating of drums. The fire drove many of the Spanish soldiers out of their huts before they could arm themselves. The noise, smoke, and flames almost totally disoriented the aroused army. Somehow, de Soto was able to grab a lance and slay one Chicasa. That was reported to be the only Chicasa to be slain in the attack.

The utter chaos and confusion ended up saving de Soto's army instead of destroying it. The engulfing flames, smoke, and noise caused the army's horses to run amok. The Chicasa mistook the horses' behavior for an attack by mounted soldiers. That caused them to call off the attack and retreat.

The Chicasa launched a second attack a few days later, but this time the Spanish were prepared. They easily repelled the attack and chased the Chicasa onto a flat plain. Once they were on level ground, the mounted soldiers had an advantage. They mercilessly massacred the Chicasa.

CROSSING THE MUDDY MISSISSIPPI

In May 1541, de Soto led his army to a low bluff about thirty miles south of present-day Memphis, Tennessee. From that point, they looked down on the vast Mississippi River. De Soto would be credited for "discovering" that great body of water. In fact, though, what he actually discovered was the inland portion of the river. The mouth of that great river had been discovered and mapped years earlier by European sailors and slave traders. Also, American Indians had known about the river long before any Europeans arrived.

De Soto saw the sweeping river as another challenge to be met. He was eager to cross over to the other side. For the rest of the month, he and his army worked at constructing rafts to take them across. Almost every day, American Indians in canoes drifted by and launched volleys of arrows

Hernando de Soto discovers the Mississippi River in this painting by William H. Powell.

at them. The men would huddle under the cover of their shields and keep working.

The attacks gave de Soto and his army new hope that the elusive golden empire was on the western side of the river. The assaults must be occurring because the Indians were trying to protect their riches. After two years of slogging through a strange new land, their goal was finally within reach.

By around mid-June, de Soto's army had constructed four large flat-bottomed rafts. On June 18, de Soto, his army, and all of their animals and supplies crossed the river.

THE EXPEDITION'S ABRUPT END

The crossing took them into present-day Arkansas. De Soto quickly had the rafts disassembled. The army marched north along the riverbank. Eventually, de Soto met some Indian traders who told him that a range of mountains to the north contained deposits of the precious metals he coveted.

De Soto sent some soldiers to investigate those claims. To his great disappointment, it turned out to be another false lead. Still, he refused to give up on his dream. He turned his army around and they marched southwest.

After several more weeks of roaming, the army settled for the winter near the site of present-day Little Rock, Arkansas. De Soto told his officers that when spring returned, they would go back to the Mississippi River and build boats to take them downstream. When they reached the mouth of that great river, they would sail on to Cuba. Then they would rest there before embarking on a new expedition.

In March 1542, de Soto began leading his army back to the river. Sometime in late April, he caught a fever. By mid-May, he was gravely ill. De Soto knew he was dying. He called his close friends to gather around him.

De Soto thanked his soldiers for their loyalty to him in spite of the many hardships that they had endured. He asked them to choose a new leader and take an oath to obey him. Then, on May 21, 1542, forty-two-year-old Hernando de Soto died somewhere on the banks of the Mississippi River.

Luis de Moscoso succeeded de Soto and led the surviving soldiers. They marched more than one thousand miles across Arkansas and Texas. However, the land became too arid and devoid of crops to sustain them. They returned to the river and built rafts, which took them 750 miles downstream to the Gulf of Mexico.

On September 10, 1543, they reportedly reached the mouth of the Panuco River near Veracruz, Mexico. It had been more than four years since they left Cuba for Florida. People who knew them had given them up for dead. None of the survivors brought back any gold.

THE LEGACY OF HERNANDO DE SOTO

Many historians have dismissed de Soto's final expedition as a futile and fruitless mission. He and his men found no great treasures and established no new colonies. Some claim that the most notable achievement was the introduction of

De Soto's followers bury him in the Mississippi River.

razorback hogs to North America. Descendants of those animals still roam some of the areas that de Soto explored.

Even his detractors would concede that de Soto was a man of great bravery and determination. He was a very skilled fighter, horseman, and military tactician. If he ever had moments where he doubted himself, he kept them to himself. He was also capable of cruel and barbarous behavior.

His explorations in southeastern America greatly increased Europeans' knowledge of the area's geography. Europeans also now recognized the Mississippi River as an important trade route for any new colonies started in the area. The written accounts of de Soto's American expedition provided a lasting record of the Indian cultures that he crushed. His explorations made it easier for Spain to establish colonies in the New World.

Unfortunately, de Soto's obsession with finding riches may make him more remembered as a

A cross was erected at De Soto Point, one of the alleged landing sites of the Spanish explorer on the coast of Florida.

ruthless treasure hunter, than as a brave explorer and military leader.

❂ EFFECTS UPON NATIVE PEOPLE

Everywhere de Soto traveled—Panama, Peru, North America—he coldly and cruelly exploited the native peoples for everything he could get. He participated in the killing of thousands, if not millions, of Indians. Thousands of Indians who were not killed in battle or by brutal treatment from de Soto and his army died from diseases carried by members of de Soto's expedition. Historian Gonzalez Fernandez de Oviedo claims that about 2 million Indians died in Panama between 1514 and 1526.

If de Soto could not satisfy the Indians with gifts and claims of friendship, he enslaved or killed them. In the case of the Atahachi, historians hold de Soto responsible for eliminating an entire civilization after the battle of Mabila. Oviedo writes that the sole purpose of de Soto's march through Florida was "neither to populate nor to conquer, but rather to disturb and devastate the land and to take away the liberty of all the natives, and not to convert or make one Indian a Christian or friend."[3]

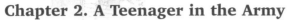

Chapter 2. A Teenager in the Army

1. David Ewing Duncan, *Hernando de Soto: A Savage Quest in the Americas* (New York: Crown Publishers, 1995), p. 20.

2. Ibid., p. 21.

3. Ibid., p. 29.

4. Ibid., p. 46.

5. Ibid.

Chapter 3. Adventures in Central America

1. David Ewing Duncan, *Hernando de Soto A Savage Quest in the Americas* (New York: Crown Publishers, Inc., 1995), p. 59.

2. Ibid., p. 63.

3. Ibid., p. 83.

Chapter 4. The Inca and the Search for Gold

1. David Ewing Duncan, *Hernando de Soto: A Savage Quest in the Americas* (New York: Crown Publishers, 1995), p. 121.

2. Ibid., p. 141.

3. John Hemming, "Pizarro, Conqueror of the Inca," *National Geographic*, February 1992, p. 104.

4. Ibid., p. 109.

5. Ibid.

6. Ibid., p. 111.

7. Duncan, p. 184.

Chapter 5. Journeying Through Florida

1. David Ewing Duncan, *Hernando de Soto: A Savage Quest in the Americas* (New York: Crown Publishers, 1995), p. 240.

2. Lawrence A. Clayton, Vernon James Knight, Jr., and Edward C. Moore, eds., *The De Soto Chronicles,* Vol. I (Tuscaloosa, Ala.: The University of Alabama Press, 1993), p. 263.

3. Ibid., p. 265.

4. Ibid.

Chapter 6. Lost!

1. Lawrence A. Clayton, Vernon James Knight, Jr., and Edward C. Moore, eds., *The De Soto Chronicles,* Volume II (Tuscaloosa, Ala.: The University of Alabama Press, 1993), p. 193.

Chapter 7. The Mighty Mississippi

1. Lawrence A. Clayton, Vernon James Knight, Jr., and Edward C. Moore, eds., *The De Soto Chronicles,* Volume II (Tuscaloosa, Ala.: The University of Alabama Press. 1993), p. 412.

2. Ibid., p. 367.

3. David Ewing Duncan, *Hernando de Soto: A Savage Quest in the Americas* (New York: Crown Publishers, 1995), p. 354.

Glossary

animosity—A bitter hostility or hatred.

armada—A fleet of ships.

befitting—Suitable or appropriate.

carnage—Massive slaughter.

conquistador—Any one of the Spanish conquerors of Mexico and Peru in the sixteenth century.

cursory—Hasty or superficial.

expendable—Able or intended to be sacrificed.

folklore—Customs, stories, and beliefs handed down among the people of a region or country.

foreboding—A sense of impending danger or evil.

garrote—To kill by strangling.

imminent—About to happen.

iron mail—Armor made of protective links or plates.

menial—Work not requiring special skills.

porter—Someone who carries baggage or supplies.

precept—A principle or rule establishing a certain standard of conduct or action.

squadron—A group of two to four troops of cavalry soldiers.

troupe—A group of actors, singers or dancers.

vanquish—To defeat or conquer as in battle.

vecino—A property-owning citizen or respected person in a town.

Further Reading

Books

Davenport, John C. *Juan Ponce de León and His Lands of Discovery.* Philadelphia: Chelsea House Publishers, 2006.

Gruber, Beth. *National Geographic Investigates Ancient Inca: Archaeology Unlocks the Secrets of the Inca's Past.* Washington, D.C.: National Geographic, 2007.

Mountjoy, Shane. *Francisco Pizarro and the Conquest of the Inca.* Philadelphia: Chelsea House Publishers, 2006.

Otfinoski, Steven. *Vasco Nuñez de Balboa: Explorer of the Pacific.* New York: Benchmark Books, 2005.

Pancella, Peggy. *Hernando de Soto.* Chicago: Heinemann Library, 2004.

Stein, R. Conrad. *Hernando de Soto: A Life of Adventure.* Chanhassen, Minn.: Child's World, 2005.

Vieira, Linda. *The Mighty Mississippi: The Life and Times of America's Greatest River.* New York: Walker & Co., 2005.

Internet Addresses

The Age of Spanish Exploration, Conquest, and Early Colonization
<http://www.artifacts.org/conquest.htm>

Hernando de Soto—Catholic Encyclopedia
<http://www.newadvent.org/cathen/04753a.htm>

Hernando de Soto—MSN Encarta
<http://encarta.msn.com/encyclopedia_761574754/Hernando_de_soto.html>

Index